everything I'll never say

Namya Saini

BookLeaf Publishing

Presentation by *BookLeaf Publishing*

Web: www.bookleafpub.com

E-mail: info@bookleafpub.com

ISBN: 9789357617611

First edition 2022

For anyone who believes they won't get their happy ending—I hope you find the strength to write your own one day

PREFACE

This book is a collection of some of the thoughts I've had over the years but never had the courage to say. These poems are the products of experiences that have shaped me and the different kinds of pain and happiness I've felt. These words—which may be trigger old wounds, habits and memories—are intended be part of a process of healing and growth, for me and for anyone who can relate to the feelings I've felt.

the elixir of Life

watching Winter extinguish the brilliant flames
that dance through the forest,
Death begins to weep.
lifting calloused palms and arms weighed down
from an eternity of lifting his scythe,
his fingers brush away tears
that stream in a shade
as unyielding as midnight.

the hunger of Time devours the leaves withering
around him,
but through his ebbing cries,
Death can hear the flirtatious sighs of Life flit
around him,
in the cry of an evening lark
as the seasons steadily change,
or the bloom of snowdrops
that shoot up from Winter's bitter grave.

it isn't until the reign of Spring
that Life stands fully before Death,
and struck by the stars perpetually dying and
blazing
in her quicksilver eyes,
they burn through the world together,

inseparable and intertwined like flames.

so long as Life laughs in honeyed tones, Death
will remain,
but within his lingering presence ignites the age
old
and aching desire
to imbue some semblance of forever
into each one of Life's dear
and fleeting breaths.

so Death bottles up his ebony tears
and places in Life's palm his gift—
the lifeblood within which the explosive delights
and passionate ends
of heroes and villains, sinners and saints
are forever instilled—

watching writers capture the flames of the forest,
before the colors crumble to ash beneath
Winter's feet,
the lovers are reassured at the sight of fingers
stained with ink,
the infinite marriage of Life and Death and the
urge to create,
blossoming across the pages as the gift of
Death's tears
breathes Life into the immortal stories of
mankind.

poetry

/ˈpōətrē/

noun

1. thinking about people who are too far away,
belonging to another time
2. dark circles under sleep lined eyes,
weary from stakeouts
trying to catch fate red-handed—
an attempt to attach some meaning
onto fleeting touches and lingering glances,
and trying too hard to wring water out of stones

3. tongues that struggle to bear the weight
of all the words left unsaid,
wanting to rip the heart off your sleeve
and leaving stale memories on repeat
as blank pages stare up at you,
their gazes heavy with everything you'll never
say

death of the old gods

they fade away in whispers,
their gilded thrones now tombs
with barren altars that crumble
alongside the mountains they once ruled.

but if you stand in their forgotten temples,
you may hear them
in the thundering crash of a wave,
the howling of a summer storm
or the melody of a gentle rain.

if you strain your eyes
and look into the night,
you may see them
in the piercing stare of a wolf
or the flowers that bloom
in spite of a phantom cold.

and if you look towards the sky
and wish upon a star,
your words breathe the slightest whisper of life
into the lungs of the dying gods.

ponding

/pänd iNG/

verb

1. clawing at life again
after listless months of suffocating on stale air,
starting to count the spaces between your
heartbeats,
believing in the haphazard sympathy of the stars,
and making wishes on melting candles
with waxy tears that drip onto healing wrists

2. following trails that lead to nowhere
and accidentally stumbling upon
sun drenched beaches, vacant playgrounds
kicking through the air, desperate to fly,
amidst the creaking of the swings
and the incessant nagging of hope

3. coaxing fires out of emptied candy boxes,
watching entangled tongues of flames
who refuse to burn to ash
but lighten hearts heavy with goodbyes
alongside the unspoken promises
slipped onto fingers aching to intertwine

4. hoping for the day to be painted
on a canvas of endless blue,
yet biking in the chatter of the rain,
efforts to stay afloat and keep treading water
applauded by an audience of thunder

5. because on those barren afternoons
when water is thicker,
and kinder,
than the blood growing stagnant
and rotting in your veins,
you dive into dewy-eyed ponds
with unwavering faith
in their murky
but vivacious depths

the wishing well

if only wishes cost pennies
cast into waters of the deepest blue,
I'd throw a couple into the well
and watch them twirl under the light of the moon

if wishes cost pennies
shimmering with the sharp taste of rust,
I'd bite my tongue and pray
until rubies burst out of my healed cuts

if wishes cost pennies
glinting with promise behind a roaring flame,
I'd strike all the matches
and watch my skin melt in the coppery blaze

if only wishes cost pennies,
the change in your pocket singing a neglected
tune,
all I'd need is a quarter
for all my dreams to come true

brand

she wanted to claw off the brand she bore,
a self inflicted punishment,
and ached to crawl out of the flesh
that kept her as a prisoner
in a jail of her own design

she desperately wanted to love
withered leaves after their flames had been
quenched
or the bitterness that coffee smeared across lips
and the dirt staining the nails of gardeners
from which flowers would never grow

because the only roses that blossomed across her
skin
where the ones she painted
in uneven strokes of crimson
and shaky breaths

seventeen

seventeen is wanting to run away from home,
ditching your friends for a boy who won't like
you back
and seeing a stranger look at you
every time you glance at the mirror

seventeen is counting all the sunsets your
summer has left,
staying up to make wishes at a quarter after
three,
lying on the pavement and talking to the stars
about all the dreams you've stopped chasing

seventeen is being surrounded by people but
feeling lonely,
living through the best and worst times,
wanting to move on to the rest of your life
but fearing how quickly the days pass by

seventeen is thinking that you know what
heartbreak is,
planning trips you'll never take,
and getting sick of the people and town that
raised you
but also wanting to stay

me before you

there's seventeen minutes left till this is over
and I can't remember the me that was before you
you've dug too deep into my soul
and I've wrecked too many of your walls
your laughs begin where mine end
and your sins are entangled with my own

time sings its final note
and the last nail is driven into the coffin
but when you smile at me,
I can see the promise of forever in your eyes

but books are kinder to read than people
because you get up and walk out the door
and I realize you ruined me,
it was me because of you
and now that you're lost to me,
who am I?

book hangover

/'bu̇k/ /'haŋ-ˌō-vər/

noun

1. reluctant fingers, the hollow feeling
of flipping to the last page,
2. half hearted wishes sinking into wells,
one last ditch at chasing love
as the moon begins to wane

3. realizing you're living on borrowed time,
wasting your words saying goodbye in different
ways
but finding the courage to brew fresh coffee
and pick up another book
because your dreams could die tomorrow,
and the only thing you have for certain
is the rest of today

three a.m.

it's three a.m.
and my friends have fallen in love
so all I can think about it is where you are,
wondering when the stardust of our atoms will
collide
and explode into the fierce flames
that will twine together our hearts

the well is overflowing with wishes,
the sky grows tired from hearing me beg
and my knees are lined with too many bruises
so make me a promise
that you'll find me in this life
and the next when this one ends

prince of darkness

as soon as their starved hounds caught the
faintest whiff
of brimstone burning through a preternatural air,
they drew a meticulous line of salt behind their
bolted doors
and told me to never let strangers in

but I wondered if the prince of darkness
was really a prince of hearts,
with scarred lips and broken wings
who wanted to brush his fingers
against any shattered fragment of life
anyone damned was willing to give him

what if the prince of darkness
was a lonesome angel
wanting to taste the world
and taste the twinkling stars,
but was tired of wishing and looking up
towards an indifferent sky

what if he was searching the night
for anyone and anyplace
that could help him find his lost will
to live, to love and to dream

enemies to lovers

kill my time and I'll kill yours
you're pointing a gun at my head
but I have a knife against your throat

if I'm poison, you're the cure
I throw my dreams up to the stars
but you've stopped believing in magic, so you don't

you're day, I'm night
I end where you begin
but sometimes your colors bleed into mine
and we end up on the same side

we lay down our weapons and call a truce,
because we can't say goodbye,
even if you're the sun and I'm the moon

you'll buy me my favorite coffee,
the kind you hate the most
and I'll let you drag me to your favorite bakery,
where pastries feel like ash in my throat
but please, whatever you do,
keep killing my time and I'll keep killing yours

sam + lily

he was sam, she was lily
and they fell for each other
fell in love, fell from grace

he was her beginning, she was his ending
and they promised to die for each other
to love, to cherish, to kill
and wreck their souls for one another

when the sun finally set on their tragedy,
and the life bled from them in pools of crimson,
she asked him if their story had been worth
a paradise lost and their names being condemned
so with his last breath, he told her the truth,
"For you, darling, I'd fall again."

crossroads

she chokes on stale dreams,
knuckles bruised and bloody from fights she's
lost,
trying to hold onto people
and memories
that have left her haunted
and lying on the floor of a glass house,
with her heart stripped and bared to the sky,
staring up at the stars that abandoned her,
she knows she's almost gone
but her story hasn't been written
and she's afraid of the silence that lies in the
dark

stumbling onto a crossroad
hazy with tendrils of a brimstone fog,
she meets a midnight stranger
with eyes that glint like a forbidden fruit
and the pavement scrapes her knees as she begs
for magic and for fresh starts
but a deal demands sacrifice
and the jagged edges of her soul smooth over
because she's known all along
that something inside her has to die
so she offers herself to the fire,

watching her skin melt away in the flames,
uncertain,
as the devil tells her she'll rise from the ashes
one day

seven deadly sins

she becomes envy,
the poison ivy snaking up
white picket fences,
bitter as she bides her time,
scorning those who've never had to drop
wishes into tight lipped fountains
or plead with an aloof sky

she becomes greed,
silver gowns dripping with opulent dreams,
robbing the stars of their light
and gold tipped wings desperate to glide
a little too close to the sun,
cheating death with each roll of the dice

she becomes sloth,
the champagne fizzling in veins
drugged by her saccharine smiles
and honey coated words,
the cloy and unforgiving taste of amber
ensnaring the tongues of false gods and liars

she becomes lust,
velvet lined silhouettes
and lips painted with rubies

that let out sultry whispers
while blood stains her hands
busy ripping out souls
and leaving a vengeful trail of hearts

she becomes gluttony,
the ravenous hunger for magic and spell binding
worlds,
frigid hands that anxiously leaf through books
devouring every piece of warmth hidden in the
silent words

she becomes pride,
jet black dresses
and kohl lined eyes
gleaming with arrogance,
and unwavering confidence in the blade she's
forged
from the visceral flames of falling too fast
and being slammed against Death's door

she becomes wrath,
a fortress of icy fury,
a blazing inferno
that the bad hands dealt by fate
can't thaw

she wears the ugliest parts of humanity on her
sleeve

but the seven deadly sins
see the old scars
and on their knees before her,
tell her a secret,
“Darling, you lived.”

waxing crescent

/ˈwaksiNG/ /ˈkres(ə)nt/

noun

1. starting from scratch,
killing the parts of yourself that you hate,
the strength to stop picking at your scars
and let your old wounds fade

2. never being the bright notes of rose and lavender
that waltz on a summer breeze
but becoming the smoke and cedar perfumed frost
faintly whispering across snow capped peaks

3. impulsive tattoos of song lyrics and snakes
coiling up trees laden with forbidden fruit,
the first sliver of hope
after a barren new moon

take me somewhere fiction

"take me somewhere fiction," she begged,
waiting for her story to begin,
but her desperate pleas fell onto deaf spines,
tight lipped as they watched
her shaking fingers thumb through well worn chapters
while the hands of Time turned the empty pages of her own life

she saw steeled hearts bound in ink
and untethered in their wills,
painted red smiles and gowns of unforgiving midnight
hiding the daggers and plots of scheming queens,
the fury of love setting villains ablaze
as they struck all the matches in the box,
dark princes dealing favors
sealed with blood stained lips
and forbidden kisses
promising to will wicked fairytales to life

she saw cities sparkling with moonlight
where dreams did not fall upon heedless ears
but rather the stars dropped down to the earth

to forests rustling with the magic
and brimming with gateways to lost worlds

so she peered up to the sky
"take me somewhere fiction," she whispered,
one last time,
and desperate to bleed some life
onto the blank pages of her story,
she closed her eyes and picked up a pen.

snow white

hope is made out of endless laughter and
polaroids,
the smell of new books and shaken espresso,
and the summer nights I've spent
memorizing the colors that dance in your eyes

hope is lacing up well worn sneakers, blush
stained cheeks
and rolled up sleeves that show off
the promises you tied onto my wrist

hope is wanting to be the princess in your love
story,
singing alongside the chatter of birds,
and being able to look into the past
and let go of everything I can't change

evil queen

vengeance is made out of lonely nights,
safety pinned hearts and broken promises,
and the sick feeling in my stomach from falling
too fast

vengeance is red bottom heels, crushed velvet
lips
and backless dresses that show off
the jagged scars from when I ripped off my
wings

vengeance is wanting to be the villain in your
love story,
painting poison onto apples
and being able to look into the mirror
without feeling afraid

stargaze

/ˈstärˌgāz/

verb

1. lying on a driveway,
tossing drunken wishes up to the sky,
telling me that you don't believe in fate
while I wonder if I've met you in a past life

2. drinking too much coffee
and spending our nights sneaking onto roofs,
admitting to me that magic might be real,
you eyes stuck on me like I'm your favorite book

3. claiming that you hate my favorite song
but still know all the words,
confessing that I light you on fire
but you like the smell of kerosene as it burns

4. vows slipping past our lips,
the only witness a waxing moon,
promising me that even when the stars go out,
I'll forever have you

we're twin flames

tell me I'm the nightmare
you want to wake up to
and that it's my brand of laughter
that's burned into your skin

tell me it's the ghost of my smile
that haunts your sleep
and that I'm the best bad decision
you've ever made

tell me you know me
like all the scars on your body
and that my name is the only prayer
that leaves your lips

and when you've run out of words to say,
tell me that you're in love
with my light, my darkness,
and every possible shade in between

www.ingramcontent.com/pod-product-compliance
Lightning Source LLC
Chambersburg PA
CBHW062205160726
48282CB00027B/1000
* 9 7 8 9 3 5 7 6 1 7 6 1 1 *